What Is the Gospel?

Crucial Questions booklets provide a quick introduction to definitive Christian truths. This expanding collection includes titles such as:

Who Is Jesus?

Can I Trust the Bible?

Does Prayer Change Things?

Can I Know God's Will?

How Should I Live in This World?

What Does It Mean to Be Born Again?

Can I Be Sure I'm Saved?

What Is Faith?

What Can I Do with My Guilt?

What Is the Trinity?

TO BROWSE THE REST OF THE SERIES,
PLEASE VISIT: **REFORMATIONTRUST.COM/CQ**

CQ

What Is
the Gospel?

R.C. SPROUL

ℝ *Reformation Trust*   A DIVISION OF LIGONIER MINISTRIES, ORLANDO, FL

What Is the Gospel?
© 2020 by R.C. Sproul

Published by Reformation Trust Publishing
a division of Ligonier Ministries
421 Ligonier Court, Sanford, FL 32771
Ligonier.org   ReformationTrust.com

Printed in China
RR Donnelley
0000620
First edition

ISBN 978-1-64289-231-4 (Paperback)
ISBN 978-1-64289-232-1 (ePub)
ISBN 978-1-64289-233-8 (Kindle)

Cover design: Ligonier Creative
Interior typeset: Katherine Lloyd, The DESK

Scripture quotations are from the ESV® Bible (The Holy Bible, English Standard Version®), copyright © 2001 by Crossway, a publishing ministry of Good News Publishers. Used by permission. All rights reserved.

Library of Congress Cataloging-in-Publication Data

Names: Sproul, R. C. (Robert Charles), 1939-2017, author.
Title: What is the gospel? / R.C. Sproul.
Description: Orlando, FL : Reformation Trust Publishing, a division of
    Ligonier Ministries, [2020] |

Identifiers: LCCN 2019033628 (print) | LCCN 2019033629 (ebook) | ISBN
    9781642892314 (paperback) | ISBN 9781642892321 (epub) | ISBN
    9781642892338 (kindle edition)

Subjects: LCSH: Gospel of Jesus Christ (1999) | Jesus Christ--Person and offices.
Classification: LCC BT203 .S668 2020 (print) | LCC BT203 (ebook) | DDC
    232/.3--dc23
LC record available at https://lccn.loc.gov/2019033628
LC ebook record available at https://lccn.loc.gov/2019033629

Contents

Chapter One

The Gospel
of God

What is the gospel? There is perhaps no more important question for us to answer, because the answer we give will help to determine our eternal destiny. Unfortunately, there appears to be widespread ignorance today among professing evangelicals about what the gospel is. What is its content? What is the good news, why is it good news, and what does it mean to believe in the gospel of Jesus Christ? We must understand not only the origin of the gospel but the meaning of the gospel. It is urgent that we Christians get the gospel right, because if we don't, we're not going to get much at all right in the understanding of the fullness of our faith in Christ.

The gospel tells us how we can be saved from our sin. If we get it wrong, we are cursed, as Paul says in Galatians 1:6–9. But if we get it right, then we can have hope. It is therefore crucial that we search the Scriptures carefully in order to clearly articulate what God tells us about how we may be saved.

That was the goal of a gathering of evangelical leaders in Washington, D.C., in February 1998. The participants at this meeting agreed that there were some serious problems in the evangelical world that reflected a disintegration of a unity that had been forged as far back as the Protestant Reformation in the sixteenth century—a unity that had remained solid for 450 years. And even though evangelical churches have had differences in theology on many points, they always maintained a sense of unity when it came to the central affirmation of the doctrine of justification by faith alone, which was regarded historically by evangelicals as essential to the New Testament gospel.

Around this time, the Alliance of Confessing Evangelicals met in Philadelphia to consider the most pressing theological issue of our day. This group agreed that the most important issue theologically was the gospel itself. As a result of the Philadelphia and Washington meetings, a unified statement of faith was drafted in order to restore unity among evangelicals, particularly in our understanding of justification.

The document is called "The Gospel of Jesus Christ: An Evangelical Celebration," and it is divided into two parts. The first part is a summation of the key points that were affirmed. It explains the gospel in the language of the laity, avoiding technical theological statements. The second part provides a statement in more precise theological language, following the format of affirmations and denials. This book will explore the affirmations and denials in order to provide a clear articulation of the message of the gospel.*

With that as our background, let's turn our attention to the statement. Affirmation 1 states:

> We affirm that the Gospel entrusted to the church is, in the first instance, God's Gospel (Mark 1:14;

---

* The full statement can be found at https://www.ligonier.org/learn /articles/gospel-jesus-christ-evangelical-celebration.

Rom. 1:1). God is its author, and he reveals it to us in and by his Word. Its authority and truth rest on him alone.

The corresponding denial reads:

We deny that the truth or authority of the Gospel derives from any human insight or invention (Gal. 1:1–11). We also deny that the truth or authority of the Gospel rests on the authority of any particular church or human institution.

This first article affirms that God is the author and owner of the gospel. In his letter to the Romans, Paul writes, "Paul, a servant of Christ Jesus, called to be an apostle, set apart for the gospel of God, which he promised beforehand through his prophets in the holy Scriptures" (Rom. 1:1–2). Paul uses the phrase "the gospel of God." Now when he speaks of the gospel *of* God, he shows us that the message of the gospel is not merely a message *about* God, though it certainly is that. But the word "of" here in the Greek means that the gospel belongs *to* God. It is His announcement. It is His message. He is the origin or the author of the gospel.

We also see a close connection between the word *author* and the word *authority*. God is the One who declares the gospel in the first place. He is the original author of it, and as the owner and author of it, He is the One who gives the gospel its abiding authority. So, the message that we've proclaimed as Christians, that we've called the *gospel*, is not an idea that some religious teacher came up with in antiquity. Even in the Old Testament, we find hints of the gospel proclaimed, and certainly the New Testament church received the gospel directly from Christ and from His Apostles. We might say that the first great Apostle of the gospel is Christ Himself, but even when Christ proclaimed the gospel, He was fulfilling the will of the Father. It was the Father who sent the Son to make this announcement. It was the Father who authorized the Son to speak it to His contemporaries (John 5:19, 30).

One of the central issues during the Reformation of the sixteenth century concerned our justification. The Reformers argued for the doctrine of *sola fide*, meaning that we are justified by faith alone, apart from works. This is often called the *material* cause of the Reformation. How we are justified is central to the gospel, and it's because of the importance of this issue during the Reformation that Protestants became known as *evangelicals*. The word *evangelical* comes from the Greek *euangelion*, which is the New Testament word for *gospel*. The Protestant Reformers were called evangelicals because they believed that in the controversy concerning the doctrine of justification, the central matter at stake was the content of the gospel itself. But behind the whole controversy was the ongoing dispute about authority.

On what grounds did Luther dare to differ from the teaching of his parent church? Luther was forced to admit publicly that in his judgment, it was possible for the pope and church councils to err. He said that he would be willing to change his stance on justification if it could be demonstrated to him that his teaching was out of sync with the Bible. For Luther, the final authority was Scripture and Scripture alone. The crisis moment came at the Diet of Worms in 1521 when Luther was on trial and called to recant his teaching. He replied with the famous statement: "Unless I am convinced by Scripture and by plain reason and not by popes and councils who have so often contradicted themselves, my conscience is captive to the Word of God. To go against conscience is neither right nor safe. I cannot and I will not recant."

In this statement, the formal cause of the Reformation was given public utterance: Scripture alone has the binding authority on the conscience of the believer. Rome argued that the authority of Scripture rests on the prior authority of the church and that the church is the one that declares the initial authority of Scripture.

Remember that the first affirmation says that God is the author of the gospel; He reveals it to us in and by His Word, and its *authority* and truth rest on Him alone. Only the Word of God has ultimate absolute authority to bind our consciences. Likewise, the denial states: "We deny that the truth or *authority* of the Gospel derives from any human insight or invention. We also deny that the truth or authority of the Gospel rests on the authority of any particular church or on any human institution." The gospel's authority rests on God and God alone.

When we declare and preach the gospel, we do so under the aegis of divine authority. We as humans cannot call anyone to believe in Jesus Christ as his or her Savior on the basis of our own authority. Rather, when we preach the gospel, we are simply messengers communicating a message that has its origin in God Himself. That's what Paul is saying at the beginning of his epistle to the Romans. Before he begins his exposition of the content of the gospel, he identifies himself as an Apostle, one who is called of God and set apart by Him, but who is giving a message that is not Paul's invention. Paul's Apostolic authority is not the message's final authority. God declares it. God owns it. God gives it its authority.

Chapter Two

Power to Save

The affirmations of articles 2 and 3 of "The Gospel of Jesus Christ: An Evangelical Celebration" are rooted and grounded in New Testament truth. Article 2 focuses on the need to look to God and His gospel for effective power in our spiritual lives. Article 3 might cause us to pause and wonder where we can find the "good news" in its affirmation.

Affirmation 2 reads:

We affirm that the Gospel is the saving power of God in that the Gospel effects salvation to everyone who believes, without distinction (Rom. 1:16). This efficacy of the Gospel is by the power of God himself (1 Cor. 1:18).

The corresponding denial reads:

We deny that the power of the Gospel rests in the eloquence of the preacher, the technique of the evangelist, or the persuasion of rational argument (1 Cor. 1:21; 2:1–5).

Paul writes: "I am under obligation both to Greeks and to barbarians, both to the wise and to the foolish. So I am eager to preach the gospel to you also who are in Rome. For I am not ashamed of the gospel, for it is the power of God for salvation to everyone who believes, to the Jew first and also to the Greek" (Rom. 1:14–16). Here Paul is explaining the meaning and the content of this gospel, and in doing so he says *it is the power of God for salvation.*

This statement is so axiomatic to historic evangelical Christianity that we might wonder why it would be necessary to make an affirmation of this sort today. Why call attention to the obvious fact that the gospel is the power of God for salvation? Why, also, must the denial in our statement repudiate the ideas that the saving power of God rests on the techniques of the evangelist or the eloquence of the preacher or the cleverness of rational argument? I think the reason such a statement is needed in our day is because we have become adept at studying marketing techniques instead of the Word of God and because we often tend to rest our hopes on programs that we think will do the job of bringing people into a state of salvation. We begin to think that the power for changing people's lives is found in our programs or in our methods, and sometimes we become so intoxicated by our techniques that we fear the negative influence of a clear and bold presentation of the gospel.

Luther warned that anytime the gospel is proclaimed boldly and with clarity, the result will be conflict. It is that conflict that many people seek desperately to avoid. At times, we do everything we can to obscure the gospel because we're afraid that its power to introduce conflict into our church will be a negative influence on our congregation. We focus on everything except the gospel, forgetting that it is the gospel to which God has committed His power and the power of the Holy Spirit.

When Paul says that the gospel is the power of God for

salvation, he's saying that it is in this message that God has committed the resources of heaven to bring about human redemption. It is God who empowers His gospel. It is the gospel that the Holy Spirit accompanies and promises to use as a means to convict the world of sin and of righteousness and to quicken people to faith and eternal life. If we pull the plug on that power and seek to substitute some other human power, we are missing the whole mission of the church.

We must be reminded again and again that if we want to see the powerful presence of God and the Holy Spirit in our churches, then we need to remember that the power is unleashed through the preaching of the gospel. Yes, there will be conflict. Yes, some will take offense. But that's the price we pay for fidelity and for the power of God to bring people to salvation.

The denial states that the gospel does not rest in the eloquence of the preacher. There's no sin in eloquence, and there's nothing wrong with preachers' seeking to improve their gifts. Seminary courses help train preachers in sound methods of public discourse and organizing content for their sermons. But we do not trust in those matters of form and eloquence as the power supply for the efficacy of the gospel. Paul writes:

For the word of the cross is folly to those who are perishing, but to us who are being saved it is the power of God. For it is written,

> "I will destroy the wisdom of the wise
>   and the discernment of the discerning I will
>   thwart."

Where is the one who is wise? Where is the scribe? Where is the debater of this age? Has not God made foolish the wisdom of the world? For since, in the wisdom of God, the world did not know God through wisdom, it pleased God through the folly of what we preach to save those who believe. (1 Cor. 1:18–21)

And later:

And I, when I came to you, brothers, did not come proclaiming to you the testimony of God with lofty speech or wisdom. For I decided to know nothing among you except Jesus Christ and him crucified. And I was with you in weakness and in fear and much trembling, and my speech and my message

were not in plausible words of wisdom, but in dem-
onstration of the Spirit and of power, so that your
faith might not rest in the wisdom of men but in the
power of God. (1 Cor. 2:1–5)

Paul hints that he may have had some impairment of
speech, but if his epistles are any indication, no one would
ever accuse the Apostle Paul of being inarticulate. In his
writings, at least, Paul is certainly eloquent. Paul mani-
fests uncanny wisdom, and the acumen of his mind and
the force of his rational argument are compelling. But
Paul didn't put his confidence in human abilities. He was
convinced that the power was not in his skill or in his technique but in God. And the things that are considered wise
by God are often regarded as foolishness by this world. So
again, what is denied here is not the value of eloquence or
evangelistic techniques or rational argument but the power
of these things to effect salvation.

In article 3, our focus shifts to the sinful state of the
human condition. Affirmation 3 reads:

We affirm that the Gospel diagnoses the universal
human condition as one of sinful rebellion against

God, which, if unchanged, will lead each person to eternal loss under God's condemnation.

The corresponding denial reads:

We deny any rejection of the fallenness of human nature or any assertion of the natural goodness, or divinity, of the human race.

The gospel is good news. It summarizes the person and work of Christ and tells us how we can receive the benefits of what Christ has done for us. How can the announcement of the universal human condition of sinful rebellion before God be part of the good news, and why would this document include such a statement? To answer that question, we can look to Paul again.

In Romans 1, Paul introduces the gospel, explains that the gospel is the power of God for salvation, and speaks of the revelation of that gospel. He later expounds on the content of the gospel. But before he gets to that, it seems as if he digresses into a discussion about the human condition of fallenness. Paul writes, "For the wrath of God is revealed from heaven against all ungodliness and unrighteousness of men, who by their unrighteousness suppress the truth" (Rom. 1:18).

Throughout Romans 1–3, Paul lays the groundwork for the need of the gospel. The gospel is a remedy for the disease that has us in such ruin. Before any doctor can cure a disease, he must first examine his patient and come up with a diagnosis. The necessary presupposition for anyone to hear the gospel as good news is to first understand the bad news, to understand why we need the gospel in the first place.

Historically, Protestant pastors and teachers have helped the people of the church understand our need for the gospel by pointing to and explaining the law of God. Until people understand the law and that we have broken the law and that we are therefore exposed to the judgment of God, there is no goodness to the news of the gospel. Many people today hear the gospel and say, "So what?" because they are dull to the precarious situation in which they find themselves as rebels before God.

At the heart of the gospel is the message of reconciliation. One of the prerequisites for reconciliation is estrangement. People don't get excited about the gospel today because they don't believe that there's any real estrangement between themselves and God. But the Scriptures—particularly Paul in Romans 2 and 3—teach that all human beings have rebelled against God. All have distorted His truth. As rebels in God's creation, we refuse to honor Him as God or to be grateful (Rom. 1:21). This is true of everyone. The whole world comes before the tribunal of God as guilty; none is righteous. Not one does good, and all have sinned and fallen short of the glory of God (Rom. 3:10–12, 23). Unless we understand that, we won't really understand the significance of the gospel.

Why is justification by faith alone so important? It's important because God is just and we aren't. The God who rules heaven and earth is a holy and righteous God who will judge us according to His perfect justice, and we are unjust. If God judges us according to His standard of justice, we will be eternally under His condemnation. Until we understand those things, the doctrine of justification seems insignificant. But if we understand that God is just and we are not just, then the question of how an unjust person can be justified in the sight of a holy and just God becomes the most important question we will ever deal with (Rom. 3:21–28). And so the denial of article 3 says we deny any rejection of the fallenness of human nature or any assertion of the present goodness or divinity of the human race.

Fifty-five percent of professing evangelical respondents to the Ligonier State of Theology survey agreed with the statement that while everyone sins a little, most people are good by nature. This view denies the reality of original sin and our need for a Savior, and it is terrifying. Anyone who believes this is resting on a house of sand and is in serious danger of failing before the judgment seat of God. The Bible tells us that we are born in sin and subject to the righteous judgment of God (Eph. 2:1–3). We are not good in ourselves, and we cannot save ourselves; we need a Savior. Because of our sin, we need the gospel.

Chapter Three

Jesus: The Only Savior

We could expect no other affirmation to meet with more resistance from the American public than affirmation 4. One could say it is downright un-American. Any claim of exclusivity to any one religion strikes at the root of pluralism and relativism. We have been inundated with the view that it doesn't matter what you believe as long as you are sincere, and that all roads lead to heaven. Is God so narrow that He requires a strict allegiance to one way? But of course the framers of our document are faithful to the unambiguous teaching of Scripture.

Affirmation 4 reads:

We affirm that Jesus Christ is the only way of salvation, the only mediator between God and humanity (John 14:6; 1 Tim. 2:5).

The corresponding denial reads:

We deny that anyone is saved in any other way than by Jesus Christ and his Gospel. The Bible offers no hope that sincere worshipers of other religions will be saved without personal faith in Jesus Christ.

Jesus declared to His disciples: "I am the way, and the truth, and the life. No one comes to the Father except through me" (John 14:6). The Apostle Paul wrote that Christ is the only mediator between God and humanity: "For there is one God, and there is one mediator between God and men, the man Christ Jesus, who gave himself as a ransom for all, which is the testimony given at the proper time" (1 Tim. 2:5–6).

A mediator is a go-between, a person who stands in the middle between two parties, usually because they are estranged or involved in some kind of dispute. Throughout biblical history, particularly in the Old Testament, several people functioned as mediators. Moses, for example, was the mediator of the old covenant. He represented the people of Israel in his discussions with God, and he was God's spokesman to the people as well. The prophets in the Old Testament also had a mediatorial function; they were the spokesmen for God to the people. They stood between the people and God, and so God would speak to or reveal Himself to the prophets. Then the prophets as intermediaries would say to the people, "Thus says the Lord." The priests of Israel and the Aaronic priesthood of the Old Testament also functioned as mediators in that they spoke to God for the people. They were intercessors on the people's behalf. Even the king of Israel was a kind of mediator because he was not ruling by his own inherent power, but he was God's representative to the people. That's why God held the king accountable to rule in righteousness according to the law of the Old Testament.

In saying that Jesus Christ is the only mediator between God and man, Paul is not denying the office of these other mediators. He is instead focusing on the uniqueness of Christ's mediatorial office in terms of the role of mediation. Christ's role as Mediator is utterly unique, and that uniqueness is found not only in His work of mediation but in His person—Christ and Christ alone is the God-man. He is God incarnate, God with us. And what does God do to bring about reconciliation and redemption between God and humanity? God the Son takes on humanity and stands in the gap to bring about the reconciliation between God and His people. In that work of mediation, particularly with the work of atonement, Christ and Christ alone has the qualifications to do what is ultimately needed to bring about reconciliation.

In his book *Cur Deus homo* (Why the God-man?), Anselm of Canterbury spelled out why it was necessary for our salvation that our Mediator be one who possesses both deity and humanity. Now what is it that makes the Christian faith unique and different from all other religions in the world? The answer is simple: it's Christ. No other religion has a divine-human mediator. No other religion in this world has an atonement that can bridge the gap between God and man. No other world leader or world religious leader ever came back from the dead. Confucius had wisdom, but he died, and he stayed dead. Muhammad is dead. Buddha is dead, and so on. But only Christ had the ability to reconcile God and man. No one else was sinless. We affirm that Christ is the only way of salvation because He alone in His person has the credentials necessary to do the work of mediation that must be done to bring about reconciliation.

People sometimes ask, "Why is God so narrow that He provides only one Savior?" People instead ought to be asking, "Why would God give any Savior to us? Why would He not just condemn us all and exercise His justice by giving us what we deserve? Why does God go to the trouble in the depths and riches of His grace to give us a Mediator who will stand in our place, who will receive the judgment that we deserve, and who will give to us the righteousness we desperately need?" People need to be careful, particularly Christians who are cavalier about the uniqueness of Christ. God is jealous for His Son. Jesus is His only begotten Son. Three times in the New Testament God is heard to speak audibly, and two of those occasions are announcements from heaven about the identity of His Son. "This is My Son; hear Him" (see Matt. 3:17; 17:5; cf. John 12:28). People cannot supplant the position that God has appointed Christ to have from all eternity, where He alone is worthy to receive glory and honor, dominion and power. God commands all men everywhere to embrace and to honor Christ. God is not going to accept a substitute.

Notice that when Paul makes the statement that there is only one Mediator, he prefaces it by saying there's only one God. This same uniqueness was declared throughout the Old Testament, where God took a very dim view of idolatry. The very first commandment was a commandment of exclusivity: "You shall have no other gods before me" (Ex. 20:3). The worship of pagan deities received the condemnation of God. He wasn't pleased with false religion but saw in it a systematic rebellion against His own glory. Paul brings these threads together. There's only one God, and God has only one Son, and there's only one Mediator between God and mankind. That's difficult for people who have been immersed in pluralism to accept, but they're going to have to quarrel with Christ and with His Apostles on this point. The Bible offers no hope that sincere worshipers of other religions will be saved without personal faith in Jesus Christ.

Some believe that practitioners of other world religions can be saved by Christ, arguing that they are in effect worshiping Him in ignorance by giving their worship to something or to someone else. To anyone who is sincerely worshipful or sincerely religious, the argument goes, God will apply the benefits of the work of Christ. The denial of article 4 states that not only is Christ necessary, but personal faith in Christ also is necessary. As Paul spoke to the Greeks at Mars Hill, "The times of ignorance God overlooked, but now he commands all people everywhere to repent, because he has fixed a day on which he will judge the world in righteousness by a man whom he has appointed; and of this he has given assurance to all by raising him from the dead" (Acts 17:30–31). There is a universal requirement placed on all people to worship Christ and to profess faith in Him.

Let's look at article 5. Affirmation 5 reads:

We affirm that the church is commanded by God and is therefore under divine obligation to preach the Gospel to every living person (Luke 24:47; Matt. 28:18–19).

The corresponding denial reads:

We deny that any particular class or group of persons, whatever their ethnic or cultural identity, may be ignored or passed over in the preaching of the Gospel (1 Cor. 9:19–22). God purposes a global church made up from people of every tribe, language, and nation (Rev. 7:9).

Article 5 affirms the mission of the church, which is defined by the Lord of the church. He commands that the church be engaged in evangelism. Evangelism is never optional for the church. Mission is never optional for the church if the church is to be obedient to the Lord, the Head of the church. He commands the church to preach the gospel to every living person.

One of the great scandals of historic Christianity is how reluctant the church has been to obey this command. Millions of people in the world today have never heard of Jesus Christ. We have not fulfilled the Great Commission. We have not done what we are obligated as the church to do.

The denial of article 5 says, "We deny that any particular class or group of persons, whatever their ethnic or cultural identity, may be ignored or passed over in the preaching of the Gospel." Various kinds of churches tend to focus on people that fit a certain mold in terms of race, ethnicity, class, socioeconomic status, cultural background, and so on. We tend to go a certain way, and we tend to focus our outreach on people like us. But the denial of article 5 states that we are not to be exclusive. We are to preach the gospel to people from every conceivable background, from every ethnic group, and from every religious group. Sometimes we will not evangelize people who are involved in other world religions because we somehow think that they are to be excluded from the outreach ministry of the church. No, the command of God to the people of God is to preach the gospel to every tongue, to every nation, to every tribe, to every living person without distinction. That is an awesome obligation and one that we have been derelict in fulfilling.

Chapter Four

Jesus
the God-Man

The deity of Christ is an essential point of the gospel. The content of the gospel as we find it in the New Testament focuses on the person and the work of Jesus Christ. And though we distinguish between the person of Christ and His work, we dare not separate them. The significance of His person makes His work valid and effectual, and in and through His work we gain a deeper understanding of who He is, so that there is an intimate connection between who He is and what He does, that is, what He accomplishes for us. This is the focus of article 6. Affirmation 6 reads:

> We affirm that faith in Jesus Christ as the divine Word (or Logos, John 1:1), the second Person of the Trinity, co-eternal and co-essential with the Father and the Holy Spirit (Heb. 1:3), is foundational to faith in the Gospel.

The corresponding denial reads:

> We deny that any view of Jesus Christ which reduces or rejects his full deity is Gospel faith or will avail to salvation.

We notice that the first thing affirmed about Jesus is that He is the divine Word. This is an explicit reference to John 1, where Christ is identified with the eternal *Logos* or Word: "In the beginning was the Word, and the Word was with God, and the Word was God" (John 1:1). Later we read, "And the Word became flesh and dwelt among us" (v. 14). This is a reference to what we call *Logos Christology*.

This idea of the divine Word or the eternal *Logos* that

John speaks of in his gospel received much attention in Christian theology for the first three centuries of church history. Those in the early church who were familiar with the traditions of Greek philosophy understood the full meaning of the term *logos* in classical Greek philosophy. *Logos* expressed the principle of transcendent coherence and order that brings everything together into a unified cosmos. For the Greeks, the *logos* was an abstract principle and was certainly not thought of as a person. John borrowed this term from the Greek philosophical culture, but he did not leave it unchanged. Rather, he poured the Hebraic concept of a personal God into the term.

We affirm the eternality of Christ and repudiate any attempts to reduce Jesus to a creature. This is further confirmed in affirmation 6, which describes Christ as coeternal and coessential with the Father and the Holy Spirit. This defines in brief the doctrine of the Trinity and calls us back to the great ecumenical councils of the early centuries, most specifically to the Council of Nicaea and the Council of Chalcedon. The Council of Nicaea, which gave us the Nicene Creed, was held because of the crisis the church faced in the early part of the fourth century concerning the teaching of a man named Arius. Arius, along with his collaborators, denied the Trinity and the deity of Christ, arguing that Christ was the first creature that God ever made and that Christ, or the *Logos*, then created the world. But even though He was the Creator of the world, the *Logos* was Himself a creature and therefore had a beginning in time, and, being a creature, He was certainly less than God.

Arius argued that this *Logos* was like God in some respects. He said the *Logos* was *homoiousios* with God, meaning "of like substance." Arius agreed that the *Logos* was like the Father in His being but said the *Logos* was not of the same *essence* as the Father. That is, He did not participate in divine being. He was not God. The orthodox parties of the church, those who held to the Trinity, condemned Arianism in the fourth century. They insisted on the use of the term *homoousios*, meaning "of the same substance." The orthodox view of the Trinity since the fourth century has been that the three persons of the Godhead are one in essence, though they are three in person. So when affirmation 6 speaks of the divine Word as being coeternal and coessential with the Father and the Holy Spirit, this is what is in view. A confession of the full deity of Jesus Christ is foundational and essential to gospel faith. One cannot look to Christ in a salvific way and at the same time deny His deity as the Arians did.

Arianism did not die out after Nicaea and Chalcedon. The Church of Jesus Christ of Latter-day Saints (Mormons) and Jehovah's Witnesses follow Arius' lead in denying Christ's deity. Though these religions place Jesus in an exalted position, they follow the Arian position by denying his coeternality or coessentiality with the Father. Mormons, for example, hold to a version of the preexistence of Christ, namely, that He existed before the world began. But they deny His eternality. There we see the connection with Arianism: God first made Christ, and then Christ made the world, so that Christ existed before the world, but He has not always been. He remains a creature—the most exalted creature, but a creature nonetheless.

Arianism created a problem not only for the church's theology but also for the church's worship. Christianity grew out of historic Judaism, and the New Testament does not repudiate the Old Testament. The Old Testament clearly prohibits the worship of any creature. To worship a creature—no matter how exalted that creature may be—is the essence of idolatry. This is one reason why the New

Testament, in books such as Colossians and Hebrews, labors so hard to refute the idea that Jesus is a supreme angel. Scripture is clear that Christ is above angelic beings and indeed is of the same divine substance as the Father and the Spirit.

Just as clear affirmation of the deity of Christ is integral to the biblical gospel, so too is a clear affirmation of the humanity of Christ. We find this in affirmation 7:

> We affirm that Jesus Christ is God incarnate (John 1:14). The virgin-born descendant of David (Rom. 1:3), he had a true human nature, was subject to the Law of God (Gal. 4:5), and was like us at all points, except without sin (Heb. 2:17; 7:26–28). We affirm that faith in the true humanity of Christ is essential to faith in the Gospel.

The corresponding denial reads:

> We deny that anyone who rejects the humanity of Christ, his incarnation or his sinlessness, or who maintains that these truths are not essential to the Gospel, will be saved (1 John 4:2–3).

If we move to the fifth century and go to the Council of Chalcedon, we find the church confessing that Christ is truly man and truly God, having two distinct natures: a human nature and a divine nature. Just as it is vital to affirm the divine nature of Christ, as the church was careful to do in the fourth century, so also it is vital to proclaim the humanity of Christ. It is in His humanity that Christ became the new Adam, becoming our human representative by submitting Himself to the law, living a life of perfect righteousness, and offering Himself as a sacrifice on the cross as an atonement for our sins. Crucial to His redemptive work was His achieving in His humanity a life of perfect sinlessness. For Him to qualify as our Savior, Jesus had to be without sin. Jesus had to live a life of perfect obedience. If He had sinned, He couldn't qualify to give an atonement for Himself, let alone for us and for our sins. We see how Christ's sinlessness is tied to the biblical concept of our redemption.

It is affirmed here that Jesus is God incarnate. We recall that "the Word became flesh and dwelt among us" (John 1:14). He is Immanuel, God with us. He is the virgin-born descendant of David. Yes, the way in which Christ came into the world was miraculous. But in terms of His human nature, He is of the genealogy of David.

The New Testament calls attention to the significance of Jesus' being David's Son yet at the same time David's Lord. And Psalm 110:1 states: "The LORD says to my Lord: 'Sit at my right hand, until I make your enemies your footstool.'" This One who came out of the root and lineage of David was at the same time David's Lord. He is called David's greater Son in biblical categories. In the New Testament, it is crucial that Christ be a descendant of David, because the messianic prophecies of the Old Testament said that the Messiah would be a king like David and would have to be from the tribe of Judah. The kingdom had been promised to the tribe of Judah as early as the patriarchal blessings that Jacob gave to his sons (Gen. 49:10). The New Testament carefully notes that in terms of His human ancestry, Jesus belonged to the tribe of Judah and was therefore qualified to be the Lion of Judah, the King of kings and the Lord of lords, fulfilling the Old Testament prophecies about the Messiah.

Article 7 states that we deny that anyone who rejects the humanity of Christ, His incarnation, or His sinlessness, or who maintains that these truths are not essential to the gospel, will be saved. This is a strong denial. It puts the whole question of salvation on the line with respect to an affirmation of the humanity of Jesus. What the framers of this document had in view was one of the earliest heresies that the church had to deal with, which is addressed in the New Testament itself: the heresy of Docetism. The Docetists, who were influenced by Greek philosophy and the negative view of the material world, denied that Jesus had a real human body. They believed it was inconceivable that a deity could ever become united with human flesh, because that which is physical is inherently imperfect. The real stumbling block to the Greeks was not so much the resurrection as it was the incarnation.

In his epistles, John takes a strong stand when dealing with the issue of the spirit of antichrist. To John and the other New Testament writers, anyone who denied the true incarnation of God and the true humanity of Jesus was of the antichrist. Because the New Testament emphasizes the reality of the human nature of Jesus, the framers of this document affirm both the deity of Christ and the humanity of Christ. We recall that article 5 affirmed that Christ is the sole Mediator between God and men, and that is because He alone is the One who bears two natures, a divine nature and a human nature.

When we look at the history of Christianity, we see that

the deity of Christ came under attack in four centuries. The fourth century saw the Arian controversy, and the fifth century provoked the Council of Chalcedon in 451. Then we saw the rise of nineteenth-century liberal theology that denied virtually all things supernatural, particularly the deity of Christ. This carried into the twentieth century. A full confession of the deity of Christ is one of the chief controversies that the church has had to deal with because of the impact of nineteenth-century liberalism in the mainline denominations of our own time. We need to be aware that we are living in one of those epochs in church history where the deity of Christ is under attack. In our zeal to affirm the deity of Christ in the face of those who would reduce Christ to merely a human being, we must be careful not to obscure the reality of His humanity. We must maintain both His deity and His humanity.

Chapter Five

The Perfect Sacrifice

At the heart of the good news of the New Testament is the message of the cross. In His death, Christ performed a work that effected reconciliation between God and all who put their trust in Christ. That is why the Apostle Paul said he was determined not to preach anything except Christ and Him crucified (1 Cor. 2:2). This is the focus of article 8. Affirmation 8 reads:

> We affirm that the atonement of Christ by which,
> in his obedience, he offered a perfect sacrifice,

propitiating the Father by paying for our sins and satisfying divine justice on our behalf according to God's eternal plan, is an essential element of the Gospel.

The corresponding denial reads:

We deny that any view of the Atonement that rejects the substitutionary satisfaction of divine justice, accomplished vicariously for believers, is compatible with the teaching of the Gospel.

An atonement is a payment for sin. It is a payment not made by us individually, as we are incapable of offering any kind of sacrifice to God that would satisfy the demands of His justice. God's character makes the atonement necessary, for He is altogether just. He is so just that He does not wink at sin or forgo His commitment to His own integrity and righteousness. The reason the gospel is good news, as we saw earlier, is because it answers the most significant dilemma that any human being will ever encounter: since we are sinners, we are not just or righteous, and God remains immutably and eternally just and righteous. So the question is, How can an unjust human being ever hope to survive the judgment of a just and holy God?

The remedy for this problem is found in God's eternal plan to provide a way of salvation for His people in such a way that their sins will be covered and that God's own justice will be satisfied. God will not negotiate His own righteousness. In the gospel, God reveals Himself to be both just and the justifier of the ungodly (Rom. 3:25–26). The critical work that is in view here is the work of Christ on the cross by which He offered an atonement for His people. This atonement offered in obedience by Christ is a perfect sacrifice that assuages the wrath of the Father by paying for our sins and satisfying divine justice.

Two words that are often discussed in connection with the atonement are *expiation* and *propitiation*. *Expiation* has to do with the removal of our sins from us. On the Day of Atonement in the Old Testament, more than one animal was sacrificed (Lev. 16). In fact, the high priest had to sacrifice several animals for his own purification before he could offer a substitutionary sacrifice of atonement to God. Then the priest laid his hands on the head of a goat—the scapegoat—and the goat was sent out into the wilderness away from the camp, away from the presence of God. This symbolized the removal of the sins of the people from the presence of God, or what we would call the remission of sin, meaning it goes away.

The Bible uses language like "as far as the east is from the west, so far does he remove our transgressions from us" (Ps. 103:12) to communicate the idea of expiation. So the removal of our sins is accomplished because God legally transfers our guilt and sin from our own account to Christ, who is our sin bearer. A crucial passage for understanding the New Testament Apostolic view of the cross is Isaiah 53, which tells us of the Servant of the Lord who bears the iniquity of His people. It pleased the Lord to bruise Him and to chastise Him by laying on Him our sins. That is expiation—our sins are transferred from our account to Christ. On the cross, when Christ offered Himself as a perfect sacrifice in our place, He took on Himself what was due to us.

In the Old Testament, violating the law of God meant coming under His curse. Likewise, when we sin against God, we come under His curse, His judgment on wickedness. If we were to face His judgment on our own, we would be openly exposed to the full measure of the wrath of God. But Paul tells us in Galatians that Christ takes on Himself the curse that we deserve (Gal. 3:13). He does that as our substitute. The curse that we deserve is borne in our stead by Jesus. This means, as the denial states, that Christ provided a *substitutionary* atonement. The price is paid by a substitute, by someone other than the actual guilty party. From a legal perspective, all of us have sinned against God and have incurred a debt, a moral indebtedness to His perfection. We are debtors who cannot pay our debts.

There is a difference between what we call a *pecuniary* debt and a *moral* debt. A pecuniary debt is the kind of debt we acquire when we owe people money. When we say in the Lord's Prayer, "Forgive us our debts, as we also have forgiven our debtors" (Matt. 6:12), we're not speaking of pecuniary debts; we're talking about moral indebtedness. My favorite illustration of this is of a little boy who walks up to the counter of an ice cream parlor and asks for two scoops of chocolate ice cream. The server gives him the cone and says, "That will be two dollars." A look of dismay comes across the face of the child as he reaches in his pocket and pulls out a single dollar bill, and he says, "But my mommy only gave me one dollar." He doesn't have enough money to pay for his cone, to pay his indebtedness. After observing this, I walk over to the server and hand her a dollar bill. Now the question is, Is the server obligated to accept that payment by a substitute? Yes. I offer legal tender on behalf of the child, and the server now must take that payment because the debt has been paid. It doesn't matter who pays the debt as long as the debt is paid in the name of the person.

But suppose the scenario were different. Imagine that I'm standing in the store and the server is in the kitchen. The little boy runs into the store, goes behind the counter, scoops two scoops of ice cream, puts them in a cone, and starts to run out the door. The server then grabs him by the scruff of the neck and says: "Hold on there, young man. What do you think you're doing?" Then she calls the police because the boy has stolen the ice cream. A police officer comes, and the server explains that she caught this little boy stealing the ice cream. After watching all this, I say: "I have the two dollars. Let me pay the two dollars, and let's forget about the whole thing." Is the server obligated to accept that payment? No. Because what we have here is not simply a monetary debt but also a moral debt. If a substitute offers to pay the consequences or the penalty for the moral debt, the one who has been offended has a choice whether to accept the substitutionary payment.

In Christ's atonement, the Father accepts the sacrifice that is given by His Son and His justice is propitiated or satisfied. While *expiation* has to do with the removal or the remission of our sins away from ourselves, *propitiation* has to do with our relationship with God. In the atonement, Christ satisfies the demands of God to God's satisfaction, which enables God to then extend the benefits of redemption to all who are represented by the One who does the propitiation, namely, Jesus.

Now, many theories of the atonement throughout church history have denied the satisfactory and substitutionary nature of the atonement. Some have reduced the atonement to simply an example of a heroic act of human self-sacrifice or an object lesson that God gives to illustrate to the world that He is serious about sin and righteousness. The denial of article 8 rejects these heretical views and affirms the substitutionary and satisfactory nature of the atonement.

After addressing the atonement, our document goes on to point out another important truth that gets to the heart of our salvation: double imputation. Affirmation 9 reads:

We affirm that Christ's saving work included both his life and his death on our behalf (Gal. 3:13). We declare that faith in the perfect obedience of Christ by which he fulfilled all the demands of the Law of God in our behalf is essential to the Gospel.

The corresponding denial reads:

We deny that our salvation was achieved merely or exclusively by the death of Christ without reference to his life of perfect righteousness.

On the one hand, our guilt and our sin are transferred to or counted against Christ instead of us. But in addition, the full measure of our salvation takes place when God transfers to our account the merit and the righteousness that Jesus gained in His own life of perfect obedience. The gospel, therefore, is not just a message about the death of Christ; it's also a message about the life of Christ. Both the life of Christ and the death of Christ are necessary for our salvation. Redemption wasn't effected because Christ came to earth on Good Friday, died, and went back to heaven. Rather, He was born of a woman, and

He subjected Himself to every point of the law from the beginning of His life to the time of His death. He is the new representative of God's covenant people, the last Adam. Just as through the disobedience of the first Adam, who represented the human race, death and all kinds of catastrophic consequences came into the world, so the New Testament speaks of the last Adam, through whose obedience we can be made well and reconciled with God (1 Cor. 15:21–22, 45).

In Christ's death, the negative judgment on sin is satisfied and fulfilled, but in His life the positive achievement of merit and righteousness is accomplished. You see, we need both. We need something that will do away with our guilt, and that's what the atonement does. But if that's all Christ performed, then that would just put us back to square one. It would give us innocence, but it would not give us righteousness. Righteousness is something that has to be achieved. And we are not able to achieve it on our own. The point is, the gospel declares that Christ died for us and that He also lived for us. He takes our guilt by imputation. He gives to us His merit also by imputation.

Faith in the perfect obedience of Christ by which He

fulfilled all the demands of the law of God for us is essential for salvation. When we put our faith in Christ, we put our trust not only in the person but also in His work, what He has accomplished in our behalf. To believe the gospel is to despair of ever living righteously enough to satisfy the demands of God's justice and instead to trust in and rely on what Christ did for us in His life as well as in His death.

Lurking beneath the explicit terms of the gospel, which declares that we are justified by faith in Jesus Christ, is the tacit assumption that justification before God is by works and by works alone. How that can be? Don't we strenuously defend the doctrine of justification by faith alone? How, then, can justification be by works alone? It is because our justification comes about through *the works of Jesus Christ*. That's what we mean when we say we're justified by faith. It's because we have faith and trust in the works that were performed by someone *other than us*. It is Jesus' works that earn righteousness and the blessing of God's promises, and it is by His good works that the original agreement that God made with mankind was fulfilled. Where Adam failed in his works, Christ was victorious in His works, and it is by His good works that we are redeemed when we place our faith in Him. In the final analysis, we will be judged by works, and we will stand before God one of two ways. Either we will stand before the judgment of God on the basis of our works, or we will stand on the basis of Christ's work. If we stand on the basis of our works, I guarantee you it will be bad news. If we stand on the basis of Christ's works, we will stand on the good news of the gospel.

Chapter Six

Resurrection and Justification

In the New Testament, when the early church proclaimed the message of Christ, it included a summary of Jesus' life that included the cross and the atonement as well as the resurrection. The phrase *He is risen* is vital to understanding the New Testament message and all of historic Christianity, as we see reflected in article 10 of the document "The Gospel of Jesus Christ." Affirmation 10 reads:

We affirm that the bodily resurrection of Christ from the dead is essential to the biblical Gospel (1 Cor. 15:14).

The corresponding denial reads:

We deny the validity of any so-called gospel that denies the historical reality of the bodily resurrection of Christ.

The first thing we see in the resurrection of Jesus is that Christ Himself was vindicated. In and of Himself, He was sinless. Death had no claim on Him because death is God's punishment for sin, and if one is utterly without sin, it would be unjust of God to punish him forever for sin. We know that Christ willingly took our sin on Himself, and the suffering He endured on the cross was not for His guilt but for ours. Yet, God declares the innocence and the righteousness of His Son by way of the resurrection. It is for this reason that the Scriptures say it was impossible for death to hold Him (Acts 2:24). Skeptics say we can't believe in the resurrection because it's impossible for anyone to come back from the dead. The New Testament places the impossibility on the other side of the ledger; it is impossible for Him *not* to come back from the dead—because He was innocent.

The second reason why the resurrection is so important to the gospel is that the New Testament announces that Christ made an atonement for our sins and that He was raised for our justification. Our justification before God rests on the work of Christ. Now suppose that He had lived a life of perfect righteousness, died, and stayed dead. We'd have no reason to believe that the sacrifice that He offered was ever accepted by the Father. But as Paul tells us in his speech on Mars Hill, the Father vindicates the Son and shows the truthfulness of His reconciling work through the resurrection (Acts 17:22–31). God bears witness that He has been satisfied by the work of His Son by raising Him from the dead.

This is a point we ought not overlook. Often, when Christians think of the resurrection of Christ, the chief benefit we look for from the resurrection is the hope it gives us that we will survive the grave. Certainly, the New Testament shows us that Christ is raised not simply for Himself but as the firstfruits of those who will participate in resurrection, demonstrating to us that God has promised to share the blessedness of Christ with all of those whom He represents (1 Cor. 15:23). We do indeed have the hope of eternal life ratified and confirmed for us by the resurrection of Jesus. But when we think of that marvelous benefit—that we will survive the grave—we ought not forget the link of resurrection to justification. The reason why we will survive the grave is because the power of the grave has been defeated by Christ in His atonement and in His life of perfect obedience. In this regard, the resurrection is inseparable from our justification and therefore is essential to the gospel.

The Apostle Paul had to deal with those who wanted to construct Christianity without the resurrection. He gives his most able defense of the true historical character of the resurrection in 1 Corinthians 15, where he addresses those who would try to have a Christianity without resurrection. Paul said if there is no resurrection, then Christ is not raised, and if Christ is not raised, then what? What are the consequences of that? He takes the premise that Christ is not raised and drives it to its logical, absurd conclusion. Why would anyone attach any significance to Christ if He were still dead? As Paul writes, if Christ is not raised, then we are still in our sins. You see, we have no reason to believe that we've been justified. We are false witnesses of

God. We are telling the world not only that Christ was raised from the dead but that it was God who raised Him from the dead. If this is not true, then our preaching and our faith are in vain. And we are of all people the most to be pitied. Those who have died have perished, and we have no hope beyond the grave.

Paul says it is foolishness to try to reduce Christianity to an ethical system that ignores the central affirmation of resurrection. During those centuries when the deity of Christ was denied (the fourth, the fifth, the nineteenth, and the twentieth centuries), massive attempts were made to deconstruct and reconstruct historic Christianity so that it omits the resurrection. I sat under a minister for many years who did not believe in the real historical resurrection of Christ. He gave it a symbolic type of significance, saying that the message of the resurrection of the New Testament is that we can get up and face the dawn of a new day with courage. That sounded more like Friedrich Nietzsche to me than it did the New Testament, so I said to him: "If Christ is dead, I'm going to sleep in tomorrow morning. I'm not going to spend another five minutes of my life as a Christian if that is a false hope." In fact, if the resurrection were not true, I would be numbered among those who are the most to be pitied because I've committed my life to serve a dead master rather than a risen Lord.

The twentieth century saw an effort to reinterpret the New Testament to mean that the significance of resurrection was an existential experience that the disciples had, where they suddenly came to an understanding of who Jesus was and what He was about. All the New Testament narratives that include resurrection appearances are only parables to indicate that the disciples saw Jesus in the cognitive sense; they now realized who He was. They did not have a real sensory experience of actually seeing with their eyes a person who had come back from the dead.

As our document says, if you deny the real bodily, historical resurrection of Christ, you have denied the very essence of the gospel, and whatever faith you have is not faith in the gospel that comes to us in the New Testament. Again, the document says we deny the validity of any so-called gospel that rejects the historical reality of the bodily resurrection of Christ.

The three qualifiers that are used in this denial are important to remember. One, the resurrection is *historical*. Two, it is *real*. And three, it is *bodily*. The affirmation says that at the heart of the gospel is the claim that Jesus of Nazareth really came back from the dead and that He came back in the same body that He had died in. It wasn't a new body. It was a changed body. It was a glorified body, but there was continuity between the body that was laid in the tomb and the body that came out of the tomb. It was a physical resurrection. It was a real resurrection that took place in space and time.

Now we will look at article 11, which focuses on the doctrine of justification. Affirmation 11 reads:

> We affirm that the biblical doctrine of justification by faith alone in Christ alone is essential to the Gospel (Rom. 3:28; 4:5; Gal. 2:16).

The corresponding denial reads:

> We deny that any person can believe the biblical Gospel and at the same time reject the apostolic teaching of justification by faith alone in Christ alone. We also deny that there is more than one true Gospel (Gal. 1:6–9).

The person and work of Christ is at the heart of the gospel. That is why so much of this document reaffirms the church's historic doctrines regarding Christ and His incarnation, deity, atonement, and resurrection. But the good news is not only about who Jesus is and what He did in history; the good news also includes the benefits to us that are derived from what Jesus accomplished—and not only the benefits but how those benefits are appropriated. That is, the gospel is also the message of how we are linked to Christ and how He then effects our salvation, how He is our Savior.

In Romans 1, the Apostle Paul announces the revelation of the gospel of God. He then goes on through several chapters to express the content of that gospel. He brings us to the central importance of the doctrine of justification because justification is the fruit of the work that Christ has accomplished for us. It is through His person and by His work that we are able to be justified in the sight of God. The idea that we are justified by faith and not by our works of the law is integral to the gospel.

The church has confessed since the Reformation that our justification is by faith alone in Christ alone. In fact, the term *sola fide*, which is the Latin shorthand for the doctrine of justification, simply means that we are justified by faith alone. To be justified by faith alone means that we are justified by placing our trust in Christ alone. The Reformers taught that faith is the sole instrument or the instrumental cause of our justification. Faith is the means by which we receive the benefits of the work of Christ; what Christ did for us is received by faith.

Article 11 states that we deny that any person can believe the biblical gospel and at the same time reject the Apostolic teaching of justification by faith alone in Christ alone. This speaks to the greatest controversy in the history of Christendom, which erupted in the sixteenth century and provoked the Protestant Reformation. The debate in the sixteenth century focused on the gospel. Those who believed the doctrine of *sola fide*, or justification by faith alone, were contending for nothing less than the biblical and Apostolic gospel. The dispute between Protestants and the Roman Catholic Church was, in essence, a dispute about what the gospel is. The Roman Catholic Church rejected and condemned *sola fide*, justification by faith alone.

When Paul addresses the Judaizing heresy in his letter to the Galatians, he writes that we are not to embrace any gospel other than the one that is set forth in the New Testament (Gal. 1:6–9). There is only one gospel, and that one gospel tells us that we are justified by faith alone. This denial states that if someone says he believes in the gospel but at the same time denies justification by faith alone, then what he believes is not the biblical gospel. Whatever else it might be, it isn't the good news of the New Testament, and it must be deemed to be bad news.

These affirmations are essential to the biblical gospel, to the true gospel, and without them, we do not have the very essence of the gospel. In our day, as in the sixteenth century, there have been serious controversies about the doctrine of justification. Much of that controversy is the result of our ignorance of the basic meaning of the doctrine of justification. This is a precarious position to be in because the New Testament links justification by faith alone inseparably with the gospel. If we don't understand justification, we don't really understand the gospel. And if we are going to preach the gospel, we must preach justification by faith alone.

Chapter Seven

Imputation

Of all the articles of affirmation in the document "The Gospel of Jesus Christ: An Evangelical Celebration," article 12 most succinctly states the difference between the historic evangelical theology of the gospel and that articulated traditionally by the Roman Catholic Church. Affirmation 12 reads:

> We affirm that the doctrine of the imputation (reckoning or counting) both of our sins to Christ and of his righteousness to us, whereby our sins are fully

forgiven and we are fully accepted, is essential to the biblical Gospel (2 Cor. 5:19–21).

The corresponding denial reads:

We deny that we are justified by the righteousness of Christ infused into us or by any righteousness that is thought to inhere within us.

After the Reformation began with the work of Martin Luther but before the Council of Trent, in which the Protestant view was anathematized by the Roman Catholic Church, there was an attempt to bring the parties together. Representatives from the Reformation group and representatives from the Roman Catholic Church met at Regensburg, Germany. They attempted to bring about a compromise and reconciliation between the two parties. And for a short period of time, it seemed to be successful— until it unraveled.

The point at which the two sides were not able to come to an agreement had to do with the question of the ultimate basis for justification. On what grounds will God declare a person to be just in His sight? The dispute focused attention on two words. The first was the word *imputation*, which was the favored word of the evangelicals. The Roman Catholic Church insisted on the word *infusion*. Before we consider the difference, we need to understand that both sides believed that in some sense we are justified by the righteousness of Christ. But the critical question became, In what sense are we justified by the righteousness of Christ? In what way or manner does the righteousness of Christ avail for our justification? To understand the difference, let's first look briefly at the Roman Catholic view.

According to the Roman Catholic Church, the beginning of justification takes place at baptism. According to the church, baptism is the means, the instrument, by which justification initially happens. The Roman Catholic Church believes that the righteousness of Christ is infused into the soul at baptism. What they mean by *infusion* is that justifying grace is poured into the soul of the believer, which is the grace of the righteousness of Christ. Then the person who receives this infusion of grace must cooperate with and assent to that grace. According to the Council of Trent, when actual righteousness inheres within the believer and that righteousness is inherent within the person, only then will God declare that person just in His sight.

When someone receives the grace of justification and cooperates with it and assents to it, the person is placed into a state of salvation, and he remains there unless or until he commits a mortal sin. A mortal sin is called *mortal* because it kills this inhering, infused grace in the soul. Once that grace is destroyed, a person has to be justified again, and the rejustification comes through another sacrament: penance. The Roman Catholic Church defines the sacrament of penance as the second plank of justification for those who have made shipwreck of their souls. Salvation is lost, and the only way it can be restored is through a fresh infusion of grace, which now comes through the sacrament of penance. It was issues related to the sacrament of penance, particularly the problem of indulgences, that provoked the controversy with Luther in the first place.

In opposition to the Roman Catholic Church, the Reformers taught that our justification is not by infusion but by *imputation*. Imputation has to do with God's legal declaration or decree by which He reckons or accounts one person's record for another. In justification, imputation is a two-way street; it goes in both directions. First, Christ takes the penalty for our sins onto Himself on the cross. In the atonement, Christ is the sin bearer. He becomes the sin bearer when God transfers our guilt from us to Him. Christ fulfills the Old Testament's ritual of the Day of Atonement. On the Day of Atonement, the high priest symbolically placed his hands on the head of the scapegoat. That symbolized the transfer or the *imputation* of the sins of the people to the goat. After the sin and the guilt were transferred to the goat, the goat was driven out into the wilderness, into the outer darkness. The idea of imputation is deeply rooted in the Old Testament sacrificial system, and on the cross our sins are transferred to Christ by God's forensic or legal declaration.

But that's only half the story of our justification. After Christ has paid for our guilt, we may be in a state of innocence, but we have no righteousness or any particular merit, and God, in the act of justification, is looking to see that His law of righteousness is fulfilled in us. Christ, as we've said, not only died for His people, but He lived for us as well. Our redemption was not accomplished merely by the death of Christ—as essential and as crucial as that was to our salvation. Again, Jesus didn't just come down from heaven on Good Friday, go to the cross, and then return to heaven. He was born as an infant, and He was subjected from the moment of His birth to the whole law of God.

His whole life was lived to fulfill the law of God at every single point, so that He earned or merited the blessing of God by His perfect righteousness. Again, in our justification, there is a double imputation. On the one hand, our guilt is imputed or transferred to Christ, and on the other, His righteousness is imputed to us.

For Rome, the instrumental cause of justification is baptism first and then later the sacrament of penance. For the Reformers, the instrumental cause of justification is faith. That is the instrument by which we lay hold of Christ and by which the merit of Christ is appropriated to the believer, so that all who put their trust in Christ then have the righteousness of Christ counted or transferred to their account. The Roman Catholic Church rejected this concept of imputation, saying that it would involve what they called a legal fiction. That is, if God made a legal declaration whereby He was going to transfer one person's righteousness to someone else, that would be fictional. It would involve God in a falsehood because it would not be based on the truth. Rome was asking, How can a just and holy God deem or count someone just who in fact isn't just? How can He declare someone righteous when that person in and of himself is not righteous? Rome saw this as casting a shadow on the integrity of God and involving some kind of compromise of His own righteousness.

The Reformers responded by saying this is a legal action to be sure, but there's nothing fictional about it. First, the righteousness that is imputed to us by faith is a real righteousness. It's the righteousness of Christ, and there's nothing fictional about His righteousness. Second, when God transfers something from one person's account to another, it is a real transfer. It is a real imputation of real righteousness to people who possess real faith. I would add that if we object in principle to the idea of imputation, not only would we have to reject the transfer of the righteousness of Christ to our account but we would also have to reject the cross, because clearly on the cross Christ is dying as a substitute for us. God is pouring His wrath on Him instead of on us because God has transferred our guilt to Christ by imputation.

Justification by faith alone is essential to the gospel. Without *sola fide*, you don't have the gospel. And the concept of imputation is absolutely essential to the doctrine of justification by faith alone. So if you don't have imputation, you don't have *sola fide*. And if you don't have *sola fide*, you don't have the gospel. Without this doctrine of imputation, you don't have the gospel, for the gospel stands or falls on this idea of the transfer of Jesus' righteousness to our account.

We often wonder about the significance of some of these doctrines for our daily lives and for practical living. There is nothing more relevant to our lives than knowing how we can stand in a saving relationship to a holy and just God. If our redemption were dependent to any degree on our own righteousness, then we would have no hope of salvation, because the only righteousness that could possibly meet the standard that God imposes on His creatures is the righteousness that was achieved by Christ. That is the truth we hear in the gospel, and that is the truth we cling to.

Chapter Eight

The Righteousness of Christ

A rticle 12 showed us that our justification is based on the imputation of the righteousness of Christ, and it is not found in any righteousness that inheres within us. At first glance, it might seem that article 13 simply duplicates what was affirmed in article 12. But the issue of imputation and the role of Christ in our justification is so central to our understanding of the gospel that the framers of the document we have been exploring felt it was necessary to be even more precise in article 13. Affirmation 13 reads:

We affirm that the righteousness of Christ by which we are justified is properly his own, which he achieved apart from us, in and by his perfect obedience. This righteousness is counted, reckoned, or imputed to us by the forensic (that is, legal) declaration of God, as the sole ground of our justification.

The corresponding denial reads:

We deny that any works we perform at any stage of our existence add to the merit of Christ or earn for us any merit that contributes in any way to the ground of our justification (Gal. 2:16; Eph. 2:8–9; Titus 3:5).

When we speak of the *righteousness of Christ*, we mean the righteousness that Christ achieved in and by His perfect obedience. Historically, theologians have made a distinction between two kinds of obedience of Christ. One is called the *passive obedience* of Christ, and the other is called His perfect *active obedience*. These terms do not find their way into this document, but certainly they lie just slightly beneath the surface and form the historical background for this statement.

Christ's passive obedience refers to His suffering the penalties of the law over the course of His life, culminating in His death on the cross. He submitted to the call of God to be on the receiving end of God's judgment in our behalf. Christ's active obedience refers to His keeping the law and perfectly fulfilling its demands over the course of His life. He displayed perfect obedience to the law of God at every point and in every detail.

When Luther spoke of the righteousness by which we are justified, he used two helpful phrases. The first is *justitia alienum*, which means a foreign or alien righteousness. *Justitia alienum* refers to a righteousness that is achieved by another. It is someone else's righteousness, not our own. The righteousness by which we were justified is that righteousness of Christ that is properly His own. It is not properly our own. We receive it only by imputation.

The second phrase Luther used was *extra nos*, meaning outside of us or apart from us. Again, the righteousness that is the ground of our justification is not a righteousness that is found in us, but it's a righteousness that is achieved for us by Christ. This righteousness is counted, reckoned, or imputed to us by the legal declaration of God as the sole ground of our justification.

Article 13 denies that any works we perform at any stage of our existence add to Christ's merit or earn for us any merit that contributes in any way to the ground of our justification. In view is the Roman Catholic concept of merit. Merit is reflected in Rome's practice of the sacrament of penance, which, as we recall, is necessary for the restoration to a state of justification for those who have committed a mortal sin. They are restored to a state of justification only after going through the various parts of the sacrament of penance, which includes such things as confession, an act of attrition, priestly absolution, and performing works of satisfaction. But the only merit that counts for our justification is the merit of Christ, and that merit is perfect, so it is incapable of being augmented or diminished. We can't add to perfection. We can't contribute anything of merit to satisfy the demands of God's righteousness that hasn't already been achieved for by Jesus in His perfect obedience.

Now we get to a tricky part. Our document makes a distinction between what we call *justification* and *sanctification*. Affirmation 14 reads:

We affirm that, while all believers are indwelt by the Holy Spirit and are in the process of being made holy and conformed to the image of Christ, those consequences of justification are not its ground. God declares us just, remits our sins, and adopts us as his children, by his grace alone, and through faith alone, because of Christ alone, while we are still sinners (Rom. 4:5).

The corresponding denial reads:

We deny that believers must be inherently righteous by virtue of their cooperation with God's life-transforming grace before God will declare them justified in Christ. We are justified while we are still sinners.

We are declared to be just in the sight of God while we're still sinners. Or, as Luther stated, we are *simul justus et peccator*, at the same time just and sinner. He meant that when a person places his faith in Christ, God declares him just by the imputation of Christ's righteousness. But our justification does not immediately destroy our sinful nature; we are justified, but we continue to sin. However, anyone who is justified is also indwelt by God the Holy

Spirit, and from the moment of justification, the Spirit begins His work of sanctification in the soul and life of the believer. So, even though we don't have to wait until we become righteous for God to declare us righteous, nevertheless we *are becoming* righteous. That process of being conformed to the image of Christ and of growing up in the fullness of Christ begins with our spiritual rebirth and with our justification.

It is important to recognize that our document does not deny that Christians are supposed to be concerned about good works. The Apostle James wrote: "What good is it, my brothers, if someone says he has faith but does not have works? Can that faith save him?" (James 2:14). The point is that our good works *flow out of* our justification and are not the *cause or ground of* our justification. The only good works that contribute to our justification are the good works of Jesus. Our good works come after justification as a consequence of that justification. Again, the document affirms that all believers are indwelt by the Holy Spirit and are in the process of being conformed to the image of Christ. We are to be growing in Christlikeness.

Importantly, article 14 denies that "believers must be inherently righteous by virtue of their cooperation with

God's life-transforming grace before God will declare them justified in Christ. We are justified while we are still sinners." The key word here is "before." Both Rome and evangelicals believe that justification involves a legal declaration. Justification occurs when God makes a legal judgment wherein He declares that a person is just in His sight. Both sides believe that. The debate concerns when and on what basis God makes such a declaration. The Reformers insisted that God makes that declaration before there is inherent righteousness in us. He makes that declaration the moment we believe, even while we are still sinners. That is the good part of the good news. We can have our sins forgiven, we can be adopted into the family of God, and we can be pronounced just by our Creator the moment we embrace Jesus, because at that moment all that He is and all that He has achieved becomes ours.

The New Testament calls us to "work out [our] own salvation with fear and trembling" (Phil. 2:12). Sometimes we get confused when we read that language because the words *justification* and *salvation* tend to be used interchangeably. It's true that in a certain sense we enter into salvation the moment we put our faith in Christ. But our final and full salvation doesn't take place until we enter into our glorification in heaven. So, part of the process of salvation is sanctification. But justification comes first. We are not working to achieve our justification. We are working to bring the fruits of that justification to bear in our sanctification.

Chapter Nine

A Life-Changing Gospel

The moment we embrace Christ with true faith, God declares us just by virtue of the imputation of Christ's righteousness. But even though we have been justified, we continue to sin. The lifelong process by which we are made holy and brought into conformity to the image of Christ, which begins at the moment of our justification, is called *sanctification*. Article 15 addresses the relationship between justification and sanctification. Affirmation 15 reads:

We affirm that saving faith results in sanctification, the transformation of life in growing conformity to Christ through the power of the Holy Spirit. Sanctification means ongoing repentance, a life of turning from sin to serve Jesus Christ in grateful reliance on him as one's Lord and Master (Gal. 5:22–25; Rom. 8:4, 13–14).

The corresponding denial reads:

We reject any view of justification which divorces it from our sanctifying union with Christ and our increasing conformity to his image through prayer, repentance, cross-bearing, and life in the Spirit.

As we mentioned in chapter 8, Martin Luther said that the justified sinner is at the same time just and sinner. He's just by virtue of the transfer of the righteousness of Christ to his account, but in and of himself he remains a sinner. At the moment we put our faith in Christ, we are not instantly cured of sinning. Luther said that when God pronounces a person just, it is as if He administers a dose of medicine that will make the patient well. But the cure is effected over time. That is, the cure of our sin is found in our sanctification, and sanctification is a lifelong process that is not completed until we die and enter into what the Bible calls *glorification*. Glorification is the conclusion to the lengthy process of sanctification.

The document we are exploring views sanctification as a necessary result or fruit of justification. It is not a possible consequence but a certain consequence. And that's important because some believe that a person can be justified and never begin the process of sanctification, that people can remain what is called a "carnal Christian" throughout their lives. I think this belief stems from the problem we often see of people making a profession of faith in Christ as a response to some kind of evangelistic outreach but then demonstrating no outward apparent change in their lives. Some people want to be optimistic and trust the profession of faith, so they contemplate the idea that they're really Christians but have not yet begun their sanctification. But historical, biblical Christianity says again that once a person is justified, he begins to be sanctified.

Certainly, someone who has been justified has experienced a significant change, a change from someone who is under God's curse to someone who is righteous in His sight. A person cannot be justified without possessing true faith. But Christians disagree about when that faith happens in relation to rebirth or regeneration. Regeneration refers to the work of the Holy Spirit by which a person is quickened from a state of spiritual death and transformed into a state of spiritual life. Some believe that a person has faith first, and then, as an immediate consequence of that faith, he is not only justified but also regenerated. That would mean two significant changes that are related to justification. As soon as a person has faith, he is a believer rather than an unbeliever, and he's now regenerate rather than unregenerate.

The Reformed faith reverses the order of these two elements of faith and regeneration. We say that regeneration precedes faith. When we say *precedes*, we don't mean chronologically; we don't mean that a person is regenerated and then fifteen years later has faith, or someone is regenerated and five minutes later has faith. We're talking about simultaneous actions. But when we look at it in terms of a logical order, we say that regeneration comes before or precedes faith in the sense that regeneration is a necessary condition, a prerequisite, for the presence of faith. Reformed theology teaches that the only way true faith can be manifested in the life of a person is if God first works a work of grace in his soul through the operation of the Holy Spirit, by which he is quickened from spiritual death to spiritual life and is therefore reborn. As Jesus said to Nicodemus, "Unless one is born again he cannot see the kingdom of God" (John 3:3).

A person who has true faith is also a regenerate person, a person who has been reborn. And that's why we see that sanctification must follow from justification: if faith is present and a person has been reborn, that means that person has been changed in his inner being through the operation of the Holy Spirit, and the process of sanctification, or growing in conformity to the image of Christ, has most surely begun.

Sanctification involves ongoing repentance. Some Christians think that the only time a Christian is called upon to repent is at the initiation of the Christian life. We have our initial response to the gospel, when we confess our sins before God and have a change of heart and mind, and we call that repentance. But our document here acknowledges that repentance is a lifelong practice. The Christian life is a penitent life, because as long as there remains sin in our lives, the need for confession and turning from that sin remains. So the initial repentance that we bring to the foot of the cross is not a once-for-all repentance. We are called to live a life of repentance, to confess our sins to Him daily, and as we grow in sanctification turn more and more away from sinful habits and actions. Ours is a life of turning from sin to serve Jesus Christ in grateful reliance on Him as our Lord and Master.

Once we are saved and in a saving relationship with Christ, our quest for righteousness is not over. It's really just begun. So often, we think the search for God as something that is concluded when we find Him, when in reality the Scriptures tell us that no man in his natural state seeks after God. We don't really begin to seek after God until God has found *us*. Our seeking after God and His kingdom is a lifelong enterprise, and it begins with our justification. We have not reached the end of the road. We haven't reached our goal yet. We are in a comfortable state of having been pronounced and proclaimed just by God, but we are still in the process of seeking conformity to His image, and this conformity occurs through ongoing prayer, repentance, the bearing of the cross, and living one's whole life in light of the presence and power of the Holy Spirit.

Chapter Ten

Saving Faith

Article 16 of the document "The Gospel of Jesus Christ: An Evangelical Celebration" considers the three elements of saving faith. Affirmation 16 reads:

> We affirm that saving faith includes mental assent to the content of the Gospel, acknowledgment of our own sin and need, and personal trust and reliance upon Christ and his work.

The corresponding denial reads:

We deny that saving faith includes only mental acceptance of the Gospel, and that justification is secured by a mere outward profession of faith. We further deny that any element of saving faith is a meritorious work or earns salvation for us.

The first thing article 16 affirms is mental assent to the content of the gospel. When Luther crystallized the essence of the doctrine of justification, much confusion about what it meant to be justified by faith alone resulted. Is simply stating "I affirm the truth of the gospel" enough to get you into heaven? Because of such confusion, it was necessary for the Reformers in the sixteenth century to look closely at the constituent elements of true saving faith.

The Reformers determined that saving faith comprises three elements: *notitia*, *assensus*, and *fiducia*. *Notitia* refers to the data or the content of the gospel. We don't believe that people are saved by faith in just anything. When the New Testament speaks about justification by faith, it has in view faith or belief in certain truths, and most importantly in a particular person. We are to believe in Christ. When the gospel is proclaimed, it has certain information about who Jesus is and what He has done: He died on the cross,

He rose from the dead, and so on. That's all part of the *notitia* of saving faith.

The second element is *assensus*, which is intellectual or mental assent. If I ask, "Do you believe that Jesus rose from the dead?" I'm asking whether you affirm in your mind the truth of the *notitia*, the content of the gospel. It is not enough to know what the gospel teaches; to have saving faith, we must also believe that those teachings are true—that this Jesus who died and was buried in the tomb actually, historically rose from the dead, and so on. If someone doesn't believe that Jesus is the Savior, if he is not convinced of the truth of that idea or if he believes that Jesus is still dead or fails to believe that His crucifixion was an atonement, then that person doesn't possess what the Bible and what the Reformers called saving faith. To be saved, someone has to actually agree in his mind that the statements about Jesus and about His work are true.

Saving faith also involves a third element. James wrote, "You believe that God is one; you do well," as the sarcasm drips from his pen. "Even the demons believe—and shudder!" (James 2:19). James is saying that it's not enough to affirm the proposition of the existence of God. The devil knows that God exists. Likewise, if you have a mental conviction that Jesus was who He claimed to be and that He died an atoning death on the cross and rose from the grave, all that does is qualify you to be a demon—because the demons knew the truth of those propositions. Though you can't be justified without mental assent, its presence does not guarantee justification. We need *fiducia*, or personal trust and reliance. When the Scriptures speak of receiving Christ or embracing Christ or coming to Christ in faith, it means not only believing that He is a Savior but also trusting Him as one's Savior. We are to rely on His work and His righteousness for our redemption. That is trust or *fiducia*.

The Bible tells us that if we believe in our hearts and confess with our mouths that Christ is Lord, we will be saved (Rom. 10:9), and on numerous occasions, the Scriptures call the people of God to make an outward profession of faith. A public profession of some kind is typically required to join a church. Unfortunately, our culture today has an idea that Christianity is a religion that is personal and private. People are reluctant to testify publicly to their faith in Christ, saying that it is a personal, private matter. Of course, Christianity is personal. I can't think of anything more personal than the bond a person has with Christ because of faith. But Christianity is *not* private. As personal as our faith may be, we have always been called as followers of God to be willing to make it clear publicly that we are servants of Christ; we get sober warnings from Jesus that if we are ashamed of Him publicly, He will be ashamed of us before the Father (Matt. 10:33). If we are unwilling to confess before men that Christ is our Redeemer, He will not confess us before the Father. So making a public confession of faith in Christ is not optional for the Christian.

Jesus also gave sober warnings to those who make a profession of faith in Him that is not honest or genuine. Our Lord says, "This people honors me with their lips, but their heart is far from me" (Matt. 15:8). Perhaps the scariest message Jesus ever gave came at the climax to the Sermon on the Mount. He said that many will come on the last day saying, "Lord, Lord did we not do this in Your name and didn't we do that in Your name?" and so on, and He said, "I will say to them: 'Depart from Me, you workers of iniquity. I never knew you'" (see Matt. 7:21–23). Our Lord warns us about the very real possibility of people giving verbal testimony to their faith in Christ while not actually having authentic faith in Christ. In other words, we are justified not by a profession of faith but by the possession of faith, and we can profess it without possessing it. That is what is in view in this article's denial; it denies that justification is secured merely by an outward profession of faith.

Let's look at this in practical terms. In America, particularly in mass evangelism techniques, after the gospel is preached, an invitation to accept Christ, sometimes called an altar call, is often given. The assumption is that if someone prays a prayer to accept Christ as his Savior and means it, then he will be redeemed. But it's possible to get people emotionally excited to the point where they may be moved to make an outward profession of faith. But the Bible does not teach that we are justified before God by the mere recitation of a prayer. We are not justified by the raising of a hand alone. Nor are we justified by walking to an altar. We are justified by faith. These practices are outward indications of a profession of faith, which may occur without the presence of true faith. But we must not assume that just because we walked an aisle or raised a hand or said a prayer that we are safely in the fold of Christ. The real requirement is faith.

Finally the denial says, "We further deny that any element of saving faith is a meritorious work or earns salvation for us." Some confusion can arise here because Jesus once said, "This is the work of God, that you believe in him whom he has sent" (John 6:29). Some people have taken that to mean that the one good work that justifies us is the work of faith. They say that there's a kind of merit that is attached to genuine faith, and therefore the distinction between faith and works collapses. Now, when you have theological discussions with people and ask, "Do you believe that faith is a meritorious work?" the majority of professing Christians know enough to say: "Of course not. My confidence is in the meritorious works of Jesus." However, we can easily harbor in our hearts the idea that there is inherit merit in our belief; we can tend to believe that God sees our exercising faith as a virtue that He rewards.

Think about why you are a Christian and someone else isn't. Is it because you've done something righteous that your neighbor has not? Most people would not publicly say, "I'm a Christian because I'm better than my neighbor." But sometimes that idea slips into our heads, and it is a deadly deception to ourselves to think for a moment that there's any merit or virtue in our coming to saving faith. Augustus Toplady had it right in the hymn "Rock of Ages" when he wrote, "Nothing in my hand I bring; simply to thy cross I cling." Faith is the receptacle by which we receive the merit of someone else, not something that gives us a claim to God's grace of salvation by virtue of some kind of merit.

In looking at the elements of saving faith, it's important to understand that our salvation is of the Lord; it rests on the grace of God and on the work of Christ. It's not our work that satisfies the demands of God's righteousness. It is only the work of Christ. Faith simply receives the merit that someone else has earned on our behalf. We have to guard against allowing the idea to creep into our minds and hearts that we are blessed of God because somehow we deserve it, somehow we have earned His good favor.

We are justified by faith, by the possession of authentic faith, and not by its mere profession. And as Christians, we are not to be ashamed of Christ. We must let people know of our faith in Him.

Chapter Eleven

Christ and Doctrine

We could score a 100 percent on a theological test about the content of the gospel and still not have true saving faith. Knowledge of the gospel—even an intellectual embracing of that knowledge—does not save us. What saves us, of course, is Christ. Affirmation 17 reads:

> We affirm that, although true doctrine is vital for spiritual health and well-being, we are not saved by doctrine. Doctrine is necessary to inform us how we may be saved by Christ, but it is Christ who saves.

The corresponding denial reads:

We deny that the doctrines of the Gospel can be rejected without harm. Denial of the Gospel brings spiritual ruin and exposes us to God's judgment.

We know that Christ is the Savior of our souls. That doesn't mean that the doctrines of Christ and the doctrines concerning the gospel are unimportant. Doctrine doesn't save us, but it is vital for spiritual health and well-being. Martin Luther commented that one of his contemporaries, Erasmus, had "attacked the Pope in his belly, but I have attacked him in his doctrine." Today it would be far more scandalous to be attacked in one's belly than in one's doctrine, because we live in an age where doctrine doesn't seem to matter much to people. On another occasion Luther was challenged because some of his followers had exhibited scandalous behavior. He admitted that many people in the Reformation movement were corrupt and a scandal to the gospel, but that this is also true in every confessing group. He noted that what they did have is *right doctrine*. Luther didn't mean that right doctrine excuses corrupt behavior. Someone can have right doctrine and still live a corrupt life, but no one can have a life that is pleasing to God if he ignores the truth of God that He has given to us in Scripture, because that's what doctrine is.

We tend to think that doctrine is an abstract list of propositions confined to the dusty halls of libraries or to the classrooms of academia that doesn't have much impact on our practical daily living. That's like saying the Bible has no impact on our lives. We may make a distinction between orthodoxy and orthopraxy—that is, between doctrine and practice—but we are not to separate one from the other because true living is supposed to flow out of a true understanding of the content that God has revealed to us in Scripture. This is certainly true when it comes to understanding the gospel.

It is important for us as Christians to get the gospel right, because the gospel is the power of God unto salvation, it is revealed to us in sacred Scripture, and it includes within it the person and work of Christ—His sinless life, His atoning death, and His resurrection. All of these things are truths that are revealed to us in Scripture, and together they make up the content of the gospel. What we've seen throughout our document is an emphasis on the specific elements that are contained within the content of the gospel.

Suppose your doctrine is wrong about the atonement. Suppose you believe that Jesus died on the cross not as an act of satisfying the justice of God in our place but merely to display Himself as a moral example. By having an erroneous doctrine of the cross, a faulty doctrine of the atonement, you have not gotten the gospel right. Your doctrine of the gospel falls with your doctrine of the atonement. If you deny the resurrection of Christ, you're not only missing the truth of that doctrine but you also don't have the gospel, because the resurrection is an essential ingredient to the gospel. If you believe in the atonement and believe in the resurrection of Christ, but you believe that in some way you have to earn the benefits of the work of Christ in order to be saved, you still don't have the gospel right, because you have missed the point as to how the work of Christ is appropriated to your life.

Some people say: "I don't need to know any doctrine. All I need to know is Jesus." The question is, Who is Jesus? The moment anyone begins to reply to that question, he has engaged in doctrine. Answering that question involves explaining one's doctrine of Christ. Christians who think they don't need to know theology have missed the point. It's not that you have to be a professional theologian or a

Christ and Doctrine

scholar, but you still have to be a theologian in the sense that you have to have some understanding of God, some understanding of Christ. You have to have a doctrine of God, a doctrine of man, and a doctrine of Christ to understand the gospel. So the question is not whether you have theology or don't have theology. The question is whether you have sound theology or faulty theology, good doctrine or false doctrine.

One of the great debates that we face in the church is over which doctrines are essential for salvation; that is, which doctrines, if rejected, mean that you can't be a Christian. The church is divided into many different denominations, all with their particular views of this doctrine or that doctrine, and that means, broadly speaking, that many points of error have infiltrated the church. Any distortion of the truth of God, of course, is a serious matter, but not all distortions are equally serious. So we make a distinction between that which is essential and that which is not essential.

Someone asked me once if I believed in the inerrancy of the Bible, and I said, "Yes, I do." And he said, "Do you believe it's essential for salvation?" I said, "No, I don't think that a person has to believe that the Bible is inspired of

God and without error in order to be saved." I would say that with respect to the *essence* of salvation, you don't have to believe the Bible is the Word of God. Does that mean that I think the inerrancy of Scripture is unimportant? No. I say we can make a distinction between the *being* of the church or the Christian and the *well*-being of the church and of the Christian. A strong doctrine of Scripture is vitally important to the well-being of the church and of the Christian, though it is not a doctrine that must be believed in order to be saved. However, is the atonement of Christ just a matter of the well-being of the Christian or of the church? No, it's more than that. That's something you have to believe in in order to be saved. This distinction between the *being* and the *well*-being of the church has been a help throughout history.

Again, as our document states, doctrine is necessary to tell us how we may be saved. Any information that we communicate about the gospel is doctrine. So if we have no doctrine, we have no understanding of the gospel. If we have no doctrine, we have no idea what we are to believe. We remember the Philippian jailer crying out in fear and panic to the Apostle Paul after the earthquake broke down his jail. He said, "What must I do to be saved?" (Acts

16:30). He was asking for information. He needed to know what the requirements were for salvation, and the Apostle told him what he needed to do in order to be saved.

The denial of article 17 states: "We deny that the doctrines of the gospel can be rejected without harm. Denial of the gospel brings spiritual ruin and exposes us to God's judgment." When the document speaks of spiritual ruin, it is referring to ultimate spiritual ruin. Someone who rejects the gospel is exposed to God's judgment.

God's offer of the gospel is not just one option among many. We have seen that many churches today give a so-called invitation at the end of a service, where sinners are invited to come forward and give their lives to Christ. I understand that people don't want to be arrogant or manipulative, but something is miscommunicated by the very language of an "invitation." In our culture, an invitation usually comes with a card that says "RSVP"; you are free to respond affirmatively or negatively to the invitation, and you can decline the invitation with impunity. But as Paul declared at Mars Hill, the former days of ignorance are over, and God now "commands all people everywhere to repent" (Acts 17:30). In the New Testament, the proclamation of the gospel comes to the world as a divine mandate.

God commands all people everywhere to embrace Christ, to embrace the gospel. To reject the gospel after hearing it is to embrace spiritual ruin and to stand exposed to God's judgment.

Studying doctrine can be dangerous business. We are told in the New Testament that knowledge puffs up while love builds up (1 Cor. 8:1), and we can have a purely intellectual interest in the study of theology or doctrine just to show the world that we've mastered the material. Our study of doctrine may be motivated by an attempt to build ourselves up in the eyes of other people, and in that sense it can puff us up with pride. That is why it's important that we understand that doctrine in and of itself has never saved anyone, but Christ and Christ alone is the Savior. We should be zealously and diligently pursuing an understanding of doctrine because that means we are diligently pursuing an understanding of the things that God has revealed to us in His Word.

Chapter Twelve

Proclaiming
the Gospel

The Great Commission is Christ's mandate to His disciples and to His church that He gave just before His ascension, when He commanded His disciples to go into all the world and preach the gospel to every living creature, to make disciples from all tribes and peoples and tongues and nations (Matt. 28:18–20; Rev. 7:9). This has defined the missionary task of the church since the first century, and it is the focus of the last article of the document "The Gospel of Jesus Christ: An Evangelical Celebration." Affirmation 18 reads:

We affirm that Jesus Christ commands his followers to proclaim the Gospel to all living persons, evangelizing everyone everywhere, and discipling believers within the fellowship of the church. A full and faithful witness to Christ includes the witness of personal testimony, godly living, and acts of mercy and charity to our neighbor, without which the preaching of the Gospel appears barren.

The corresponding denial reads:

We deny that the witness of personal testimony, godly living, and acts of mercy and charity to our neighbors constitutes evangelism apart from the proclamation of the Gospel.

I once spoke with a missionary who had been laboring in a remote part of the world, ministering to a group of people who had never seen a person from the West before. The missionary labored with this tribe for several years, and when they finally came to an understanding of the gospel, many were converted to Christ—including the chief of the village. On one occasion, the chief asked the missionary how long ago Jesus lived on the earth. The missionary tried to find a way to communicate in the language of the people the vast distance of time of two thousand years. There was no way she could communicate that until they talked about generations. The chief then took some sticks, and he had each stick represent a generation. He asked, "Did Jesus live during my generation?" and the missionary said no. Then he took a second stick, and he said, "Did He live during my father's life?" No. And then a third stick: "My grandfather's life?" No. And with each stick that he put on the ground, his countenance grew more and more distressed. When he finally had a length of sticks on the ground stretching all the way back to the first century, he was beside himself, and he asked, "If Jesus lived so long ago, why is it that we are only hearing about Him now?"

Unfortunately, we have not been as faithful as we ought to be to the Great Commission of Christ. There remain many people on the planet today who have never heard the name of Christ. There is perhaps no generation with less of an excuse to fulfill the Great Commission than ours, because the world has become so much smaller than it ever was in the past. We have great ability to travel, with many modern conveniences and modes of transportation.

Affirmation 18 reminds us that Christ commands His followers to proclaim the gospel to all living people, evangelizing everyone, everywhere.

Some people today react negatively to evangelism. They think that people ought to mind their own business and not try to influence other people to leave whatever religion they're in and to embrace Christ. In fact, many churches tacitly assume that certain people or groups are out of bounds for evangelism. Therefore, many of us are passive or restrictive in our outreach and don't fulfill our mandate to preach the gospel to all people everywhere.

Not only do we fail at the international level, but we fail to fulfill the Great Commission even at the local level, where we live. The command is to proclaim the gospel to everyone everywhere and to disciple believers in the fellowship of the church. The mandate of the Great Commission is not merely to proclaim, but it is also to educate or to disciple. Jesus said to preach the gospel *and make disciples*. A disciple is a learner or a student, and that means that after people respond to the gospel, they are called to be deeply involved in the life of the church because the church exists not only to proclaim but also to ground the converts to Christ in a deep understanding of the things of

God. The early church distinguished between catechetical instruction and proclamation. People who responded to evangelism were then brought into the fold of the church, and that began their nurture and discipling as students and followers of Christ.

Affirmation 18 goes on to say, "A full and faithful witness to Christ includes the witness of personal testimony, godly living, and acts of mercy and charity to our neighbor, without which the preaching of the Gospel appears barren." This section of article 18 speaks about different ways to bear witness to Christ. In the New Testament, there is a difference between *evangelism* and *witnessing*. Christians today tend to use the term *witness* as a synonym for the verb *evangelize*, as if they were interchangeable.

To bear witness to Christ is to call attention to Him in many different ways. We do it by the example that we seek to set with godly living. We seek to bear witness or to make manifest the presence of Christ through deeds and acts of mercy: by feeding the hungry, giving shelter to the homeless, and participating in other charitable endeavors. Those are different kinds of witnessing, but they are not all evangelism. Evangelism is one form of witnessing, but not all witnessing is evangelism. We bear witness to the lordship of Christ in many ways, one of which is the proclamation of the gospel.

Why do we emphasize this? It's important because people say: "I do my evangelism by my example. I don't ever proclaim Christ with words. I proclaim Christ with my life." What can your life tell people about the content of the gospel? They can look at you from now until kingdom come and still know nothing of the atonement of Christ, the resurrection of Christ, or the doctrine of justification by faith alone. How can anyone read that simply by watching your life? Your godly example may result in someone asking, "Why do you live the way that you live?" That may be the occasion for you to explain the gospel to them. But your example of godly living itself will not communicate the gospel to people. Sometimes we make an excuse for remaining silent and not proclaiming the gospel to people, saying: "I'm not going to push my views on others verbally. I'll wait until they respond to my stellar example." We also must admit that few of us are so far along in our sanctification that the world is knocking on our door, asking what makes us so special and begging us to tell them how to get it.

On the other hand, if we show no concern for the basic daily needs of our neighbors and all we do is preach to them about Jesus, our preaching will sound barren to them. Yes, it is through preaching that God has chosen to save the world, and it is the gospel that God uses as His power to bring people to Christ. But the New Testament warns us: "What good is it, my brothers, if someone says he has faith but does not have works? Can that faith save him? If a brother or sister is poorly clothed and lacking in daily food, and one of you says to them, 'Go in peace, be warmed and filled,' without giving them the things needed for the body, what good is that?" (James 2:14–16).

What kind of witness is it if we just tell people to be warmed and be filled? That is a barren witness. The denial of article 18 states: "We deny that the witness of personal testimony, godly living, and acts of mercy and charity to our neighbors constitutes evangelism apart from the proclamation of the Gospel." I think most of us can see how our bare example of living is not evangelism. The church is to be engaged in meeting people's worldly needs in terms of food and clothing and relief and employment and other acts of charity and mercy, but no content of the gospel is communicated simply by handing someone a loaf of bread or a cup of cold water. The recipient still does not know the gospel.

The other kind of witnessing mentioned in article 18's denial is the giving of personal testimony, which is people's story of coming to faith and what has happened to them as a result of their having become a Christian. This is an important part of communicating the things of God to people, and there's great value to personal testimony. But personal testimony is not the gospel. God has not promised that our personal testimony will not return to Him void. God has not chosen the power of our personal testimony as the means by which He will save the world. Our personal testimony indirectly talks about Christ but specifically talks about us and our particular situation, and it may or may not relate to whoever we're communicating with. But the gospel relates to everyone. The gospel is objective, compelling truth, and that's what we are to proclaim.

The document we have been examining, "The Gospel of Jesus Christ: An Evangelical Celebration," ends with this statement:

As evangelicals united in the Gospel, we promise to watch over and care for one another, to pray for and forgive one another, and to reach out in love and truth to God's people everywhere, for we are one family, one in the Holy Spirit, and one in Christ.

Centuries ago, it was truly said that in things necessary there must be unity, and in things less than necessary there must be liberty, and in all things there must be charity. We see all these gospel truths as necessary.

The point of this concluding commitment is this: though people of a wide diversity of faiths and denominations were involved in creating this document, and though they recognized that theological issues can still divide us on various points, they were united by the gospel. This is the necessary point on which Christians can come together in fellowship. For it is the true gospel as given to us in God's holy Word and the gospel alone that saves.

About the Author

Dr. R.C. Sproul was the founder of Ligonier Ministries, founding pastor of Saint Andrew's Chapel in Sanford, Fla., first president of Reformation Bible College, and executive editor of *Tabletalk* magazine. His radio program, *Renewing Your Mind,* is still broadcast daily on hundreds of radio stations around the world and can also be heard online. He was the author of more than one hundred books, including *The Holiness of God, Chosen by God,* and *Everyone's a Theologian.* He was recognized throughout the world for his articulate defense of the inerrancy of Scripture and the need for God's people to stand with conviction upon His Word.

Get 3 free months
of *Tabletalk*

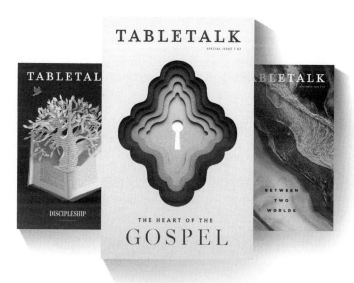

In 1977, R.C. Sproul started *Tabletalk* magazine.
Today it has become the most widely read subscriber-based monthly
devotional magazine in the world. **Try it free for 3 months.**

TryTabletalk.com/CQ | 800.435.4343